PIZZA!

For Bob
Pizza King of Connecticut

VIKING
An imprint of Penguin Random House LLC, New York

First published in the United States of America by Viking,
an imprint of Penguin Random House LLC, 2022

Visit us online at penguinrandomhouse.com.

Library of Congress Cataloging-in-Publication Data is available.

Manufactured in China

ISBN 9780425291078

10   9   8   7   6   5

TOPL

Book design by Greg Pizzoli and Jim Hoover
Set in LTC Twentieth Century Pro and Lolita

This book was printed in four spot colors: sweet-tomato red, fresh-basil green,
greasy-cheese yellow, and charred-crust black.

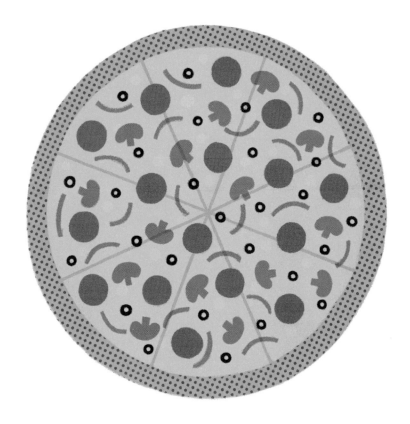

This is pizza.

And this is pizza.

french
bread
pizza

And so is this.

mini
bagel
pizza

And yes, even this is pizza.

pizza with
pineapple

This is a pizzeria.
That's a place that sells pizza.

This is a **pizzaiolo**.
That's a person who
makes pizza.

This is a **pizza rat**.
That's a rat who
likes pizza.

In the United States of America,

we eat 350 slices of pizza every second.

All over the world, people love pizza.

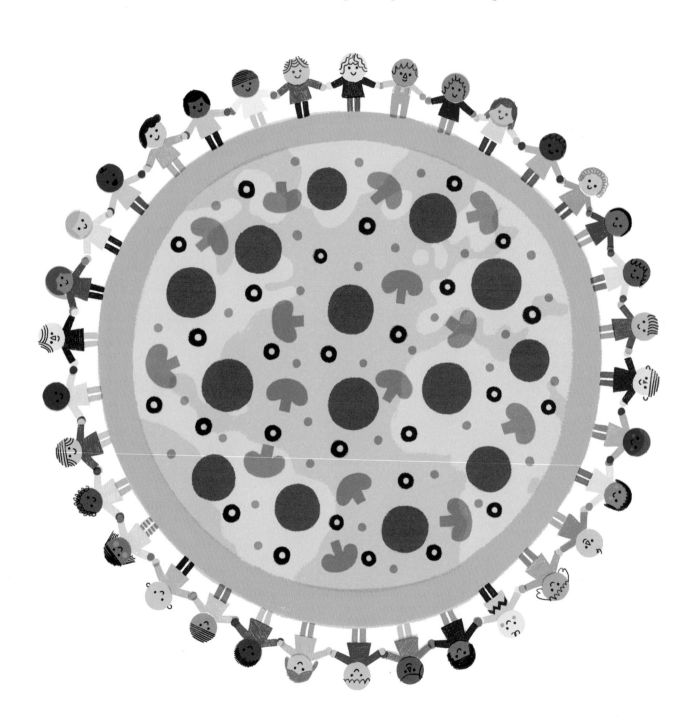

But where did it start?
When did it happen?
Who made the first pizza?

Some people
say it started in
ancient Greece.

The Greeks would cook a flatbread topped with olives and honey, which they called plankutos.

But is that pizza?

Um, no.

Others say it was the Persians.
The soldiers of Darius the Great
would cook a shallow crust
directly on their shields.

Pretty cool, sure.
But is *that* pizza?

the GOLDEN apple

Actually, the tomato
DOES NOT come from Italy.

Tomatoes are thought to be
originally from Peru, and didn't
come to Europe until the 1500s.

SS POMODORO

For centuries, most Europeans thought tomatoes were unhealthy—even *poisonous*—and many people refused to eat them.

But in Naples, Italy, people did cook with tomatoes.

They added tomatoes to many Italian recipes, including a dish they called pizza.

This is
RAFFAELE ESPOSITO.

He made dough with flour, yeast, water, sugar, olive oil, and salt. He topped the dough with tomatoes and cheese.

Then he cooked the pizza in an oven heated with burning wood.

He was famous for making
the best pizza in Naples.

In 1889, King Umberto and Queen Margherita visited Naples,
and they heard about the amazing pizzas by Raffaele Esposito.

The story goes that Queen Margherita
asked Esposito to bring her some pizza.

Esposito came up with three different pizzas, and the queen loved them all, but her *favorite* was topped with tomatoes, mozzarella cheese, and basil leaves.

The colors look a lot like the Italian flag, don't you think?

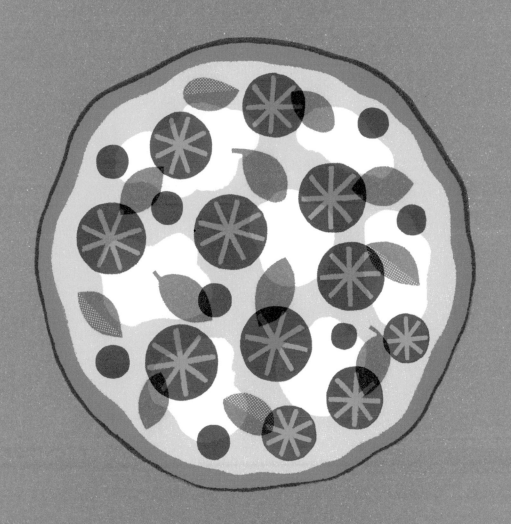

Esposito named this pizza after the queen, and still today we call it Pizza Margherita.

The popularity of pizza
soon spread across Italy.

And when Italian immigrants
moved to the United States,
they brought their love of
pizza with them.

Between 1880 and 1924,
four million Italians moved
to the United States.

Aren't you glad they did?

This is

GENARRO LOMBARDI.

Many people think that his pizzeria
was the first in New York City.

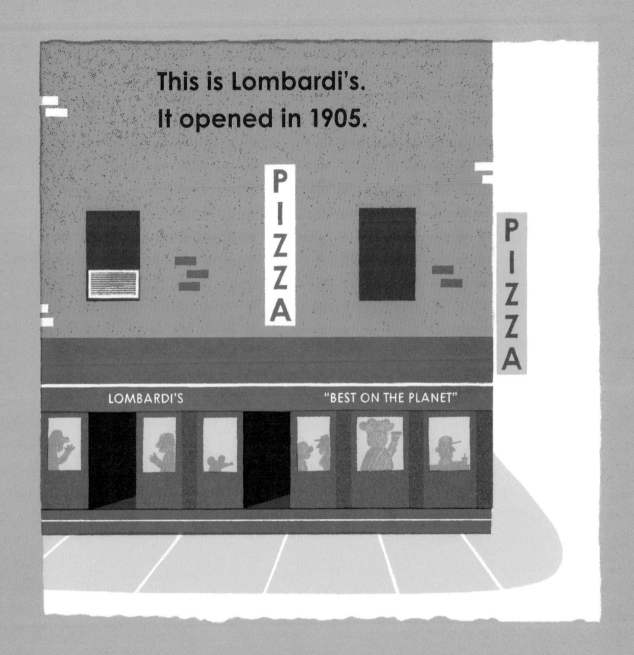

This is Lombardi's.
It opened in 1905.

Have you ever been there?

American soldiers returned home from Italy, and they brought back a hunger for pizza.

Soon pizzerias had opened all over the United States, and each region found a way to make their pizzas unique.

NEW YORK

New York pizza is considered by many to be the American pie. It's known for large slices, chewy cheese, and a thin, flexible crust.

CHICAGO

Chicago-style pizza is very thick and often called "deep dish" because of the deep pan in which it is cooked.

PHILADELPHIA

Philadelphia may be best known for cheese-steaks, but they also make a unique pizza they call "tomato pie." It has no mozzarella, just a sprinkling of pecorino cheese.

DETROIT

In Detroit, they bake pizza in a rectangular metal pan, which gives this style a distinctive shape and crispy, chewy texture.

CALIFORNIA

California-style pizza has a crust similar to pizzas in New York, but the toppings—including barbecue chicken, goat cheese, eggs, and even avocado—are what makes California-style pizzas really special.

PAY HERE

TIPS

PIZZOLI'S
PIZZA

"PIZZA WITH A SMILE"

What is pizza like
where you live?

Today, people make pizza all around the world, and they all make it their own way. Different cultures make pizzas with unique doughs, sauces, and toppings.

In Sweden, they make a pizza topped with curry powder, peanuts, and bananas!

In Brazil, it's not uncommon to see green peas on pizza!

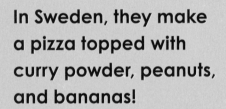

In Japan, people sometimes top their pizza with mayo jaga—a combination of potato, bacon, and mayonnaise.

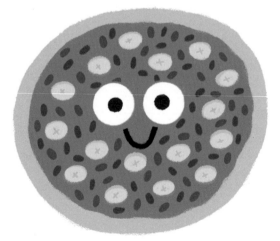

Did you know that Hawaiian pizza is actually from Canada? It's true! It is topped with pineapples and ham.

In Russia, they enjoy a pizza topped with four kinds of fish—served cold!

If you ever visit Costa Rica, you should try a pizza topped with shredded coconut!

I'll try any pizza once!

Right now, somewhere in the world,

someone is enjoying a pizza.

Are you?

Pizzoli's Mini Pizzas! Toaster-Oven Style

Grab a grown-up and follow these instructions to make four mini pizzas in just about fifteen minutes!

INGREDIENTS

- Two English muffins
- 1 cup shredded mozzarella cheese (optional)
- 1/4 cup tomato sauce
- Anything else you want for toppings!

1 Preheat your toaster oven to 375 degrees.

2 Split the English muffins in half so that you have four mini pizza "doughs."

3 Place the four English muffin halves on the toaster oven baking sheet, crumbly side up. If you don't have a baking

sheet, you can also use aluminum foil. This will keep the crumbs from dropping down into your toaster oven.

4 Lightly toast your English muffins in the toaster oven—but just for a minute or two. This is to make them nice and crispy.

5 Use a spoon to add a dollop of tomato sauce to each of the four muffin halves. Use enough sauce to cover the top of the muffin, but not too much, or it will make your pizza soggy.

6 Sprinkle cheese over the tomato sauce. If you'd like to make this a vegan pizza, you can use nutritional yeast instead of cheese, or simply leave it out altogether for a mini tomato pie!

7 Add any other toppings you'd like. But remember, when it comes to toppings, less is usually more.

8 Bake the mini pizzas in the toaster oven for ten minutes or until the cheese is melted.

9 Let the pizzas cool for one minute.

10 Enjoy! Congratulations, you are now officially a pizzaiolo!